Original title:
Quips in the Quercus

Copyright © 2025 Creative Arts Management OÜ
All rights reserved.

Author: William Hawthorne
ISBN HARDBACK: 978-1-80567-430-6
ISBN PAPERBACK: 978-1-80567-729-1

The Humor Hidden in the Bark

The tree stands tall with secrets inside,
Laughs that echo where shadows reside.
Crowned in leaves, it tickles the air,
Branches chuckle without a care.

Squirrels debate who's stealing the show,
"Not me!" they cry, as acorns fly low.
Riddles wrapped in twirling vines,
Nature's jest in its grand designs.

Woodland Whimsy

In a grove where breezes quake,
Even the mushrooms giggle and shake.
Frogs wear glasses, discussing their plans,
While hedgehogs dance in their tiny pants.

The brook sings tunes of witty delight,
Fish splash around, causing a fright.
Each beetle sports a comical grin,
In this forest, the laughter won't thin.

The Oak's Gentle Mockery

With leaves that whisper in playful tease,
The old oak leans on a whimsied breeze.
"You think you're bold?" it chuckles and swings,
"Watch me dance, as the sparrow sings!"

Mice are jesters, with tails held high,
Cracking jokes as they scurry by.
Beneath its branches, the stories unfold,
Of nutty pranks and mischief untold.

Jokes Between the Twigs

Twigs huddle close, sharing a laugh,
As the wind blows by, they take a half.
"Why did the leaf refuse to play?"
"It couldn't take root, so it fled away!"

The branches gossip about the moss,
"How did it win? Oh, what a toss!"
Bouncing ideas from sap to bark,
In a forest alive with humor's spark.

Sarcasm Under the Skies

The clouds are just a cover, it's clear to see,
They roll their eyes at gravity, oh so carefree.
Stars winking in jest, giving night a spark,
Fools dance on rooftops, leaving their mark.

Sunlight laughing, casting shadows in play,
Trees whispering secrets, come join the fray.
Nature's got humor, wrapped in a breeze,
Life's a grand jest; can we take it with ease?

Barking Up the Right Tree

In the forest of jests, where trunks stand tall,
Bark tells a story, amusing us all.
Squirrels gossip loudly, not caring who hears,
With nutty punchlines that elicit cheers.

Branches stretch wide, a perfect perch for wit,
Swinging from humor, every heart stays lit.
A woodpecker tapping, a drum of delight,
In this playful realm, we dance in the light.

Revelations from the Oak

An oak stood firm with tales up its sleeve,
Proclaiming wise cracks, who'd dare to believe?
Underneath its canopy, laughter takes flight,
With whispers of folly that brighten the night.

The acorns drop down, shattering the gloom,
Echoes of chuckles replacing the doom.
Roots intertwining, a joke shared in jest,
Nature's own stand-up, it's simply the best.

The Laughing Lattice of Leaves

Leaves rustle softly, a tapestry bright,
Mimicking laughter, infusing the night.
Wind tickles branches, a playful caress,
Each gust brings a giggle, a whimsical mess.

Colors collide in a whimsical dance,
Every fluttering leaf has a chance to prance.
Nature's own chuckle, a symphony true,
Finding fun in the quirks of every hue.

Whispers of the Oak Grove

In the shade where laughter blooms,
Squirrels plot their nutty dooms.
Leaves giggle with a rustling sound,
As critters dance upon the ground.

Mice in suits play poker games,
Cheeky crows call out their names.
Acorns tumble, roll and bounce,
While bees buzz in a merry flounce.

Rabbits crack their silly jokes,
As dripping sap delights the folks.
A wise old owl serves tea and cake,
Under branches where the giggles wake.

Nature's banquet, full of fun,
Sunshine winks, and shadows run.
With every breeze, the spirits lift,
In the grove, there's always a gift.

Jests Beneath the Canopy

Beneath the boughs, the shadows play,
Where wise old trees have much to say.
A beetle boasts of flying high,
While ladybugs just laugh and sigh.

Twigs gossip about squirrels' tricks,
In their antics, we find quick flicks.
A raccoon juggles acorn treats,
And everyone joins in their tweets.

The sun peeks through with rays of gold,
As fuzzy bumblebees share tales bold.
The grass hums softly with its tune,
While crickets chirp 'neath the bright moon.

Underneath the leafy cloak,
Each laugh's a story that we stoke.
In this great hall of bark and leaf,
We find our joy, a sweet relief.

Tales from the Timberline

At the edge where woodlands meet,
A fox spins yarns about his feet.
He prances near the bubbling brook,
And playfully gives the frogs a look.

Bumblebees debate their stings,
While owls hoot of forgotten things.
The breeze brings whispers of a time,
When tree trunks danced in perfect rhyme.

Frolicking fawns trade funny tales,
Of mischief caused by mischievous snails.
The nightingale croons songs of cheer,
As laughter rings from far and near.

Each twist of root holds secrets tight,
Where humor sways in soft moonlight.
In this timberland, joy runs free,
A comedy born from each grand tree.

Echoes of the Leafy Realm

In the heart of branches wide,
Frogs wear crowns and take a ride.
Ducks don hats and stroll about,
With laughter ringing, full of clout.

Squirrels write a daily spree,
On pages found in every tree.
Mice hold meetings, make a plan,
For cheese that's huge, as only they can.

Birds play bingo on high wires,
While woodpeckers satisfy their desires.
Echos float like bubbles in air,
Filling the woods with joyful flair.

With each rustle, stories thrive,
In this leafy world, we come alive.
Here's to the laughter, the light, the cheer,
In the realm of leaves, we hold so dear.

Japes in the Emerald Oasis

The frog in the pond wore a tiny top hat,
And croaked out a tune, imagine that!
His dance made the lilies giggle with glee,
As fish swirled around, sipping iced tea.

A beetle complained of the heat and the sun,
While ants rehearsed for a race just for fun.
A snail boasted slow, 'I'm fast with my slime,'
And the rabbit just laughed, 'You're slow all the time!'

Mirth by the Gnarled Roots

Under the branches, a party took shape,
With squirrels in suits, and a wise owl drape.
The hedgehogs played darts, 'I'll win this, you'll see!'
And the raccoons judged, 'An acorn for free!'

A fox told a joke, though it fell rather flat,
When a rabbit yelled back, 'Stop it! And scat!'
But laughter erupted, the night bright and clear,
As each little critter let go of their fear.

Whimsy in the Whispering Woods

A lizard wore glasses to read his old book,
While a crow on the branch just wanted to cook.
They plotted a feast with a dash of delight,
But the antelope said, 'It's still bright outside!'

With moonlight our chef, good flavors will soar,
Together they giggled, 'Let's cook up some lore!'
So pies made of petals and nectar on plates,
Drew a crowd of amused, festive forest mates.

Smiles in the Shaded Grove

In a grove where the sun beams were dancing with trees,
A bear wobbled by, dripping honey, oh please!
The bees buzzed around, saying, 'not so precisely!'
While the raccoons rolled laughing so very nicely.

The turtles in tune made a band with great feel,
While frogs played the drums, giving quite the peel.
A party took off, with laughter and cheer,
As every small creature spread joy far and near.

Chatter Among the Canopies

Squirrels debate on acorn worth,
While birds giggle at their mirth.
Leaves gossip softly in the breeze,
Telling tales of sneaky bees.

A raccoon jests with a wily grin,
Mouse in a top hat, ready to spin.
The sun chuckles, casting its glow,
A comedy show in nature's flow.

The branches sway, a friendly cheer,
As nature's laughter fills the sphere.
Grasshoppers leap with a playful tease,
While frogs croak jokes with perfect ease.

Under the shade, a playful band,
Join the fun, take a stand.
As leaves dance wildly in delight,
A comic feast, a joyful sight.

The Oak's Unseen Smile

Beneath the bark, a grin does hide,
Whispers spread from side to side.
Rabbits chuckle, their tails a-flop,
As the oak shares a witty top.

The branches creak, a voice so sly,
"Oh look," it says, "the clouds waltz by!"
Gophers roll in the soft, green grass,
With every joke, the moments pass.

A wind's joke makes the leaves shake,
While ants plot pranks for fun's own sake.
Tickled trunks with laughter ring,
The oak stands proud, a jester king.

Beneath the shade, the laughter brews,
As time drifts on, the fun renews.
Every rustling leaf a sign,
That nature's humor is simply divine.

Woodland Whispers of Wit

In a grove where the shadows play,
The owls hoot secrets by night and day.
A witty fox in a cape of rust,
Shares puns that crumble leaves to dust.

The stream giggles, tickling the stones,
While frogs contemplate their silly tones.
Mushrooms chuckle, sprouting in lines,
Each a wiseacre with playful designs.

The trees conspire in leafy chats,
Swaying gently, these merry brats.
A laugh erupts from a hidden nook,
Where crickets dance, and the owls look.

Every rustle is a joke retold,
In these woods, where humor unfolds.
The sun sets low, but the smiles stay,
In this woodland world, where laughter plays.

Frolicking in the Foliage

Through branches thick, the giggles fly,
While butterflies flit and clouds roll by.
Beneath vast canopies, spirits rise,
With every joke, joy fills the skies.

In leafy lanes where shadows dance,
Even moths take a chance to prance.
A blender of bliss in every hue,
Sharing tales of things they'd do.

An old tortoise with wisdom vast,
Cracks a joke that leaves all aghast.
The laughter spills like morning dew,
While chipmunks clap, in glee accrue.

The forest echoes with playful cheer,
As every critter draws near.
In this realm of foliage so grand,
The dance of humor is truly planned.

Jokester's Haven in the Woods

In the shade where shadows play,
Squirrels trade their nuts for hay.
A fox tells jokes with clever grins,
While birds join in with chirps and spins.

The tree trunks laugh, a sturdy crowd,
With whispers soft, they're feeling loud.
A raccoon juggles acorns with flair,
As laughter dances in the air.

The owls roll eyes from branches high,
With wisecracks hooted, oh my, oh my!
Each rustling leaf's a giggle shared,
In this haven where hearts are bared.

So come and join this merry spree,
Where woodland creatures sing with glee.
In quips and riddles, fun's the rule,
A jocund joy takes every fool.

Revelries of the Leafy Sanctuary

Underneath the leafy dome,
The critters gather, far from home.
A raccoon cracks a witty line,
While fireflies flash, a glow divine.

Squirrels boast of nutty feats,
While hedgehogs roll, on curved little seats.
Each bark's a joke, each root a laugh,
As laughter's measured by the half.

The wise old trees declare a jest,
With branches shaking, they're feeling blessed.
Frogs croak tunes, a symphonic din,
While fish join in, a splashy grin.

Here in this nook where mischief thrives,
Giggles blossom, the spirit survives.
A sanctuary of jokes galore,
With nature's humor, we all crave more.

Frolics in the Forested Paradise

In the glen where sunbeams beam,
The creatures dance, a joyful theme.
A turtle tells a slow-paced tale,
While wildflowers giggle in the gale.

The bumblebees buzz a funny tune,
As chipmunks twirl, beneath the moon.
Leaves rustle with a secret laugh,
As creatures plot their merry craft.

The brook babbles with puns so sweet,
With stones that dance, skipping on their feet.
A party grand, beneath the pines,
Where every creature twirls and shines.

So raise a toast with acorn caps,
To mirth and mayhem, to joyful laps.
Here in this paradise of fun,
The frolics never cease, not until we're done.

Cheer in the Crowned Canopy

Beneath the crowns of leafy cheer,
The woodlands buzz, the mood is clear.
A weasel makes a cheeky play,
While laughter heralds the coming day.

The crows exchange their witty quips,
As field mice share their secret tips.
The branches swing like a jolly swing,
While laughter's echoes start to cling.

With wisecracks woven in the breeze,
The forest thrives with jesting trees.
A dappled light adds to the fun,
As woodland mischief has begun.

So join the frolic, don't delay,
In this canopy where glee holds sway.
The beauty here's a punchline bright,
In nature's arms, all feels just right.

Silliness Among the Serene Stems

A squirrel wore a tiny hat,
With acorns tucked in just like that.
He danced around the tall pine tree,
Singing songs of glee, carefree.

The robin laughed at the poor chap,
Who stumbled on a root, fell with a flap.
But up he got, with graceful flair,
Claiming he just meant to do a dare.

The breeze tickled the leaves above,
Nature's giggle, a playful shove.
Beneath the branches, shadows play,
In this silly world, who needs a ray?

The sun peeked down with a cheeky grin,
Joining in the fun, where to begin?
All around, laughter filled the air,
In this green realm, joy is everywhere.

Jestful Journeys in the Greenery

A rabbit wore mismatched shoes,
Hopping about, he couldn't lose.
Chasing butterflies, round and round,
Each leap a giggle, a joyful sound.

Along came a tortoise with a wink,
"Your shoes are silly! What do you think?"
The rabbit grinned, "They're my best flair,
Perfect for style, beyond compare!"

They ventured deep where secrets nest,
Finding treasures, no time for rest.
With every twist, they shared a jest,
In this green world, it's all a quest.

The trees chimed in, with leaves that shook,
Their laughter echoed, you could just look.
As dusk drew close, they found their way,
Through the meadow where giggles play.

Glee in the Grassy Interlude

A ladybug spun in the air,
Said, "I'm a dancer! Do you dare?"
The grass stood tall and began to sway,
As critters gathered for the ballet.

A frog croaked low, a silly tune,
While fireflies twinkled like stars at noon.
With every hop, the joy would spread,
Even the flowers nodded their heads.

The sun peeked in with a ray of cheer,
"Let's gather round, bring laughter near!"
So they twirled and twisted, side by side,
In the grassy field, joy was their guide.

With every laugh, the echoes soared,
Creating a melody even bored.
In this moment, they felt so free,
A silly gathering beneath the tree.

Amusements from the Ancient Arbor

An old oak said, "I'm wise, you see,
But here's a joke: what's a tree?"
"Leaf it to me!" yelled a cheeky sprite,
They chuckled so loud, it felt just right.

The wind responded with a playful whir,
As branches jostled, all to concur.
"Let's play hide and seek!" called a spry hare,
"Whoever finds me needs hidey flair!"

Around the trunk, they dashed and darted,
With giggles of joy, they never parted.
Beneath the shade, shadows grew long,
In this merry madness, they felt so strong.

As twilight drew in, laughter rang clear,
Turning the woods into a cheer sphere.
Armed with joy from the day's delight,
They'd meet again, beneath moonlight.

Uproarious Understories

In the shade of the branches, whispers giggle,
Leaves flutter like laughter, oh what a wiggle.
Squirrels conspire, plotting their fun,
Stealing acorns, oh what a run!

Wise old owls crack jokes from high,
While chipmunks chuckle as they run by.
Nature's own stand-up, full of glee,
Every rustle's a punchline, just wait and see!

A deer trips over a root with a thud,
Makes it look graceful, so he feels good.
The breeze carries chuckles, so light and sweet,
In the leafy realm, laughter's a treat!

The ants march along, in a comical way,
Marching to tunes of their own cabaret.
With every misstep, they scramble and tumble,
Nature's own jesters, never to fumble!

Witty Winks from the Wild

The brook babbles secrets, witty and sly,
Fish flip with flair, as they splash and fly.
Rabbits dance round with a comic delight,
While fireflies twinkle, joining the night.

A woodpecker drums out a silly refrain,
Barking up jokes, driving others insane.
With each peck of the beak, the punchline's revealed,
The forest's a stage, and humor is wheeled!

The fox sneaks up, with a wink of his eye,
Chasing his tail as the birds laugh nearby.
Every twist of his whiskers, a jest in the sun,
In this playful patch, joy's never outdone.

Under the canopy, the laughter flies free,
In a world full of whimsy, just come and see.
Amidst leafy giants, hilarity flows,
Nature's own comedy, where no one outgrows!

Timeless Tales of Timber

Once was a tree, stood sturdy and tall,
Boastful of tales, it knew them all.
From how squirrels jumped with acrobatic flair,
To the time the sun hid without a care.

Beetles parade in a dramatic show,
Waving their tiny flags, down below.
Each knot in the bark carries laughter untold,
Whispers of stories in the wood so bold.

The summer breeze teases, tickling the bark,
With a rustling giggle that lights up the dark.
The roots tell of mischief, buried in soil,
A history of hilarity, eons of toil.

Beneath the broad canopy, legends abound,
Where laughter echoes and joy can be found.
Timber's old humor, a playful embrace,
In every ring of the tree, a smile's trace!

The Oak's Cheery Chortle

An oak stood proud, with branches spread wide,
Chortling with laughter, it couldn't hide.
The acorns dropped, with a comedic plop,
Sending critters scurrying, the giggles won't stop!

Breezes carried mirth through each leafy spire,
Rustling the branches, like a joke on a wire.
A raccoon rolled by, slipping on a pine,
With every misstep, he turned to divine!

The shadows danced, in a whimsical way,
As the sun set low, at the end of the day.
Every critter gathered, for a laugh and a cheer,
In the oak's sturdy arms, all worries disappear!

So come gather round, in this forested bliss,
Lift your spirits high, for comedy's kiss.
With every bark echoing joke after joke,
The oak's never grumpy, it's more like a bloke!

Sassy Chats in the Leafy Lounge

Under the branches, chatter flows,
Sassy remarks in the wind that blows.
A squirrel winks, a bird does tease,
Nature's gossip in the rustling leaves.

In the shade, a rabbit grins,
Sharing stories of clever wins.
With every flutter, a laugh we share,
A leafy lounge beyond compare.

The acorn drops with a witty thud,
As raccoons strut, all covered in mud.
The trees chuckle, and so do we,
In this vibrant, jolly jubilee.

With each rustle, a joke awaits,
In the canopies, where humor elates.
Join the whispers, take a seat,
In this lounge where the fun is sweet.

Joyful Shenanigans of the Woodland

In the forest, a dance takes flight,
Creatures twirl from morning to night.
A fox with flair, a deer with style,
Every prance and leap makes us smile.

Beneath the boughs, the mischief brews,
Rascally rabbits sing silly blues.
The owls hoot their raucous cheer,
While squirrels plot some nutty queers.

Near the stream, a frog leaps high,
Crafty quips, as they hop by.
Laughter echoes across the glade,
In joyful shenanigans, we parade.

So join the romp, don't be shy,
The woodland welcomes the curious eye.
With every rustle, the woods come alive,
In this joyful place, we truly thrive.

Whispers of the Oak

Under the oak, secrets abound,
In soft whispers, laughter's found.
Leaves curl and chatter, gently sway,
As the forest teases throughout the day.

A wise old owl with tales to tell,
Of pranks and plots that went quite well.
The breeze carries jokes from branch to branch,
In the shade, who wouldn't dance?

Squirrels gossip in the sunlit beams,
Dreaming up mischievous schemes.
And every rustle, a chuckle shared,
In the oak's embrace, none are scared.

So take a seat in nature's chair,
Join the whispers that fill the air.
With every leaf and twig's delight,
The peace of laughter makes it right.

Echoes in the Canopy

In the canopy, echoes play,
Lively notes from dawn to day.
Chirps and giggles fill the space,
A tree-top show, a joyful race.

With every swing, the branches sway,
And little voices sing and say,
"Join the fun, let spirits lift,
With nature's humor, it's the best gift."

The breeze carries tales of the wild,
Where every creature is playful and mild.
A hedgehog rolls with charming flair,
In this vibrant dance, we all share.

So climb up high, don't miss the show,
The canopy beckons, come and go.
In this echoed laughter, we all meet,
Where humor and nature form a beat.

Playful Shadows on the Ground

In the park where shadows dance,
A squirrel twirls, in a leafy trance.
He throws nutty jokes, quite absurd,
While birds chuckle and flip, undeterred.

The sunbeams slip through branches tight,
Creating shapes that bounce in light.
A turtle smirks on a sunny stone,
Claiming it's a throne, all on his own.

Laughter bubbles from the creek,
As frogs croak puns with daring cheek.
Each rustling leaf joins in the game,
In this woodsy world, none feels the same.

So if you wander, pause a while,
Listen closely, and let it beguile.
For nature's giggles swirl around,
In playful shadows, joy abounds.

Banter Beneath the Boughs

Amidst the oaks with trunks so grand,
A gaggle of geese takes a stand.
They honk and gab, a raucous crew,
Blabbing tales of whacky views.

The rabbits join, with ears so tall,
Sharing stories that boggle all.
A hiccuping hedgehog steals the show,
With tales of adventures in the snow.

The crows caw back, with sass and might,
Trading jabs from morning till night.
It's a comedy club beneath the green,
Where every critter plays their scene.

So take a seat, enjoy the jest,
Nature's humor is truly the best.
With laughter echoing through the trees,
Beneath the boughs, let your heart seize.

Sassy Squirrels and the Oak's Charm

High in the branches, they plot and scheme,
Sassy squirrels, the woodland team.
With acorn hats and tails held high,
They might just hatch a nutty lie.

One leaps and lands with a dramatic flair,
A daring stunt in mid-air — beware!
The oak below shakes its mighty limbs,
As if to say, 'You're far too grim!'

With cheeky grins, their stunts unfold,
Chasing sunlight, so brave, so bold.
They throw down puns like acorns tossed,
For every giggle, a branch is crossed.

So here's to the charm, with humor bright,
These furry jesters, a sheer delight.
In every leap, a story we find,
Sassy antics that tickle the mind.

Nature's Punchline

In the woods where laughter blooms,
A wise old owl crafts clever tunes.
With feathers ruffled, he tells a tale,
Of a wise old fox who chased his own tail.

The bees are buzzing, their jokes alight,
"None can match our dance in flight!"
They spin and twirl through flowers fair,
Making honeycomb dreams fill the air.

Down by the stream, fishes quip,
With gurgling voices, they never skip.
"It's a real catch when we weave our lines!"
Nature's punchlines crackle as time unwinds.

So heed the whispers of each living thing,
For giggles abound in the songs they sing.
In nature's woods, humor takes flight,
A cheerful world painted with light.

Banter Among the Boughs

Underneath the leafy green,
A squirrel told a joke unseen.
The owl hooted, 'Not so sly!'
While crickets chirped their alibi.

A chipmunk planned a daring heist,
To steal a nut, but thought twice.
The acorn blinked an eye in fright,
'Good luck, friend, it's quite a sight!'

The fox pretended to be sly,
But tripped and fell, oh my, oh my!
The laughter echoed through the trees,
Even the breeze chuckled with ease.

So gather 'round, let spirits soar,
With tales and jests, who could ask for more?
In this tall wood, absurd and free,
Life's punchlines hang from each sturdy tree.

Merriment in the Forest Shadows

In the shade where critters creep,
Bunny dreams and badgers leap.
The hedgehog rolled with giggles low,
While the grasshoppers put on a show.

A wise old tree with bark so bold,
Whispered secrets from days of old.
The saplings snickered, small yet spry,
'With roots like ours, we'll surely fly!'

A raccoon played a prank so grand,
With funny hats made from the land.
The forest floor erupted in glee,
As laughter danced from tree to tree.

So if you're ever lost or gray,
Seek the shadows where the jesters play.
With each new giggle, joy will bloom,
In this merry wood where fun finds room.

Witty Words in the Woodlands

Beneath the boughs of whispering leaves,
A fox recounted tales that tease.
Each pun was sharp, each jest was bright,
A tapestry of laughter light.

A family of owls shared a wise old quirk,
Making shadows dance with every smirk.
The toad croaked jokes, a ribbiting sight,
Lighting up the dusk with sheer delight.

With a thump and a thud, the raccoon fell,
Claiming it was just a 'furry spell.'
The chatter grew louder, as leaves took flight,
In this woodland realm of pure delight.

So let the woodsman take a cue,
Join in the laughs that spring anew.
For in the heart of nature's play,
Witty words will lead the way.

Laughs Under the Arboreal Arch

Under the arch of leafy schemes,
The critters hatched their comic dreams.
The hedgehog laughed, 'A spiny show!'
While raccoons danced with gleeful flow.

A bird dropped in with feathered grace,
Claiming it could win a race.
'I'll fly high, you plod along!'
But tripped on branches, oh so wrong.

With acorns tossed like balls of cheer,
The laughter rang for all to hear.
'It's just a game!' cried out the hare,
Who juggled nuts with frantic flair.

So when you wander through the grove,
Look for the humor, let it rove.
In the bark and barkers, find your spark,
And create your own laughs in the dark.

The Vibrant Veil of Humor

In the shade where branches sway,
Squirrels chatter, come what may.
A wig on the ant, just a jest,
Nature laughs, it knows what's best.

A fox in shoes, what a sight!
He prances around, a delight.
With twigs for ears and a grin,
It's clear who's winning this hilarious spin.

A turtle starts a race so sly,
While the rabbit just walks by.
Each giggle shared among the trees,
Echoes softly with the breeze.

With fallen acorns as a crown,
The critters dance and twirl around.
In this wood, joy takes its toll,
A world where laughter fills the soul.

Nature's Snickers

In meadows sunlit and bright,
Daisies gossip, what a sight!
A butterfly's dance, oh so grand,
Tickles the daisies, isn't that planned?

The raccoon dons a bandit's flair,
Stealing snacks without a care.
A cackle comes from behind a bush,
As the deer joins in, all in a rush.

Owls hoot jokes from high above,
In the trees they share their love.
A punchline wrapped in a hoot,
It's not just wise, it's quite astute.

Nature's chuckles fill the air,
With gossip that's beyond compare.
In this vibrant green domain,
The laughter echoes, never in vain.

Under the Oak's Watchful Eye

Beneath the branches, tales unfold,
Of chipmunks brave and stories bold.
A crow tells knock-knock jokes to the mouse,
While the rabbit hides in a leafy house.

An ant juggles crumbs with flair,
While ladybugs stop and stare.
The beetles tap a tiny beat,
As laughter dances on tiny feet.

The fox rolls over in the grass,
Admiring how the fun won't pass.
A breeze whispers secrets, so warm,
Encouraging smiles and playful charm.

Under the oak, lives a jest,
Where every critter feels quite blessed.
With whispers soft and giggles low,
In the heart of nature, joy does grow.

Woodland Wit

In the wood, a wise tree stands,
Holding secrets in its hands.
A squirrel cracks a joke so sly,
Even the sun cracks a smile in reply.

The mushrooms giggle on the ground,
As the tortoise hums a silly sound.
With patches of sunlight on the floor,
Nature's humor opens every door.

A fox with shades struts with flair,
While crickets play tunes in the air.
With each note, the leaves respond,
As laughter spreads, a magic bond.

In every nook, where shadows play,
The woods hold jokes, brightening the day.
With every rustle, a snicker goes,
In this land of giggles, anything goes.

Fables of the Wooded Whisper

In the shade where shadows play,
A squirrel jokes the day away.
With acorn hats and nutty puns,
He tickles all the woodland runs.

The owls hoot a silly tune,
Underneath the laughing moon.
With wisdom wrapped in feathered glee,
They share their quirks, just wait and see.

The rabbits hop in merry spry,
Trading jests that make clouds fly.
Each tale another twisty plot,
Where laughter blooms and worries knot.

A fox slips in with clever grin,
Pretending he's a regal kin.
The trees all giggle at his flair,
For nonsense dances in the air.

Playful Phrases in the Thicket

The bushes buzz with giddy chat,
Where everyone's a friendly brat.
A hedgehog shares a prickly jest,
While nearby bees take up the quest.

The dew drops wink with cheeky light,
And tease the mushrooms, oh so bright.
Each blade of grass offers its wit,
In this glade where laughter's lit.

A toad croaks jokes with croaky charm,
No need for quiet, bring the alarm!
The crickets chirp in quick refrain,
And join the chorus, all in vain.

So when you wander through the green,
Expect the quirks you've never seen.
For nature's jesters frolic near,
In every rustle, snicker, cheer.

Lighthearted Laughter by the Old Tree

Beneath the boughs of ancient style,
The bark erupts in laughable smile.
Each branch a stage, each leaf a cheer,
The wood is ripe with humor here.

A raccoon dons a mask so sly,
Pulling pranks that catch the eye.
His antics leave the stumps in glee,
As laughter echoes, wild and free.

An old owl cracks an age-old joke,
The kind that makes the silence choke.
His wisdom calls for joyful cries,
While critters roll with teary eyes.

So gather round the sturdy oak,
And revel in that gentle yoke.
The chuckles dance with every breeze,
Creating memories that tease.

Quirks of the Canopied Space

In the treetops, giggles soar,
As squirrels plot their cheeky lore.
A wily fox, with tail askew,
Claims every branch, claims every view.

The ravens caw in mock debate,
On who's the silliest of the late.
Their cackles rise in joyous flight,
Through the canopy, pure delight.

A dappled fawn with spots of grace,
Trips and tumbles in this embrace.
While flower petals fall like rain,
Each stumble fuels the laughter train.

Let's toast to fools, let's toast to trees,
Where whimsy dances with the breeze.
In every nook, a story's spun,
Of playful hearts, and endless fun.

Oak Tales with a Twist

In the shade of ancient bark,
Squirrels plot with plenty of spark.
One says, 'Let's steal that pie!'
The other shrieks, 'But it's too high!'

A rabbit hops by, ears all a-flop,
Sings, 'If we climb, we might just drop!'
The acorns wink from their leafy beds,
Laughing softly, filling their heads.

A wise owl hears the chatter below,
Twirls a twig, puts on a show.
'What's the fuss? It's just a snack!'
The leaves rustle back, 'Now, that's a quack!'

So the trees laugh, their branches sway,
In this lighthearted game they play.
Each giggle adds to the forest sound,
Where whimsy and wonder are always found.

Chuckles from the Canopy

From above, the branches creak,
The critters chuckle, play hide and seek.
A crow caws, 'What's the game today?'
A squirrel shouts, 'We'll dance and sway!'

The woodpecker taps a joyful beat,
While foxes shuffle their tiny feet.
'Join us up here, it's a sight to see!'
The conifers whisper, 'Can we join free?'

A breeze swirls laughter, round and round,
As mushrooms giggle beneath the ground.
'What's so funny?' a daisy demands,
'It's the weevils, they're doing their hands!'

So the canopy sings, a chorus bright,
Echoes of mirth in the dappled light.
Nature's jesters in a leafy array,
With joy that dances through each sunny day.

Echoes of Ecstasy in the Timber

In the timberland, what fun we find,
As critters gather, so sweetly entwined.
A porcupine grins, 'I've got a joke!'
A raccoon replies, 'Make it quick, don't choke!'

The rabbits laugh under a shady tree,
'What did the leaf say to the bee?'
The answer buzzes, floating so clear,
'You're all pollen, but I'm just here!'

A brook laughs softly with a rippling sound,
As fish wiggle in the watery ground.
'Is that all you've got?' a frog croaks wide,
'I'll jump so high, I'll even glide!'

So echoes of joy weave through the air,
With giggles and snickers everywhere.
In this realm where all creatures mingle,
The heart of the forest begins to tingle.

Leafy Laughter

Beneath the leaves, they giggle and play,
From dawn till dusk, they brighten the day.
A chipmunk chimes in, 'What's the best snack?'
'Nutty brownies!' the others shout back!

In the grasses, the ants march in tune,
Singing of picnics under the moon.
'What's in our basket? Oh, what could it be?'
'A crustacean, or just some green peas?'

A tale unfolds with each passing breeze,
And the butterflies dance with the highest ease.
They flutter and flitter as they tease the air,
For moments like these, they simply do care.

So gather around in the light and shade,
For the laughter of nature can never fade.
With every rustle and tickling giggle,
They remind us to play and simply to wiggle.

Nature's Mischievous Mind

In the shade where whispers grow,
Squirrels plot with seeds to throw.
Bees hum tunes of silly prance,
While frogs in ponds begin to dance.

The breeze plays tricks on leaves so green,
Tickling branches, a playful scene.
Rabbits in hats, oh what a sight,
Making shadows leap with delight.

Beetles boast in their tiny cars,
Racing quickly beneath the stars.
Witty owls with glasses ask,
"Who dressed the trees? It's quite the task!"

Nature laughs in vibrant hues,
As flowers gossip with the blues.
Every rustle and swaying vine,
Holds tales of folly, so divine.

Merriment of the Meadowlands

In fields where daisies polka-dot,
Bunnies giggle, oh what a plot!
A partridge struts, feathers all a-fluff,
Chasing butterflies, oh such fun stuff!

Sunbeams tickle the dandelion heads,
Caterpillars grinning in their thread.
Ladybugs sport their tiny crowns,
As grasshoppers wear their finest gowns.

From honeyed blooms, the nectar flows,
While crickets compose with funny prose.
A wise old owl gives a knowing glance,
Saying, "Every critter loves to dance!"

So let the meadows cheer and sing,
For life is bright as an emerald spring.
Laughter echoes across the land,
Spreading joy like grains of sand.

The Oak's Comedic Chronicles

Beneath the oak, the tales unfold,
Of nutty acorns, brave and bold.
Swaying branches play peek-a-boo,
While roots tickle toes, just for you.

Mice in boots, they take a stroll,
Chasing shadows, achieving their goal.
A squirrel juggles its winter stash,
As wind gusts by, they make a splash.

"Be yourself!" the oak tree shouts,
"Life's too brief for silly doubts!"
With every leaf, a joke takes flight,
Bringing laughter, pure delight.

So gather 'round, let stories bloom,
For nature's stage dispels the gloom.
Each giggle whispers from the bark,
Making magic, igniting a spark.

Radiant Ridicule in the Glade

In a glade where shadows play,
The rabbits tell jokes in a cheeky way.
A jester fox with a twitchy tail,
Shares silly tales that never fail.

The plants all chuckle with vibrant cheer,
Trading quips that all can hear.
Every breeze holds a secret jest,
As sunbeams dance, inviting the rest.

A turtle remarks, with a slow, wise grin,
"Fast is fun, but slow's where you win!"
The daisies burst with petals loud,
As laughter dances through the crowd.

So join the fun beneath the trees,
Where nature's humor flows like these.
In the glade of joy, let's celebrate,
Because laughter's the best antidote—just wait!

Snickers in the Shade

In the cool embrace of leafy greens,
A squirrel is plotting and it seems,
He's stashing acorns all around,
While giggling at what he has found.

Beneath the branches, laughter spills,
Birds chirp, swapping their playful thrills,
One says, 'Did you see that fellow?
He thought he'd blend in with the yellow!'

A fox trots by with a wry little grin,
'Those leaves are for hiding, not a din!'
The laughter rises like the midday sun,
Even the bugs seem to join in the fun.

Oh, the whispers of mischief float in the air,
As creatures find joy without a care,
In the shade where shadows play games,
Nature's laughter has no names.

The Oak's Cheeky Charm

An oak tree stands with a knowing wink,
His bark so rough, yet leaves so pink,
He sways just right when the breeze is near,
'Come closer friends, I won't bite, I swear!'

The rabbits hop by with curious flair,
'Did you hear that? It's full of snare!'
The oak chuckles deep, a belly-shake laugh,
'Not a trap, just a chance for a half-baked gaffe.'

Dancing fawns and frolicking mice,
Spinning tales of tumble and twice,
'It's a dance party,' the oak declares,
'Join in, my friends, let go of your cares.'

Underneath where the sunbeams chime,
Every creature revels in hilarious time,
Together they bask, beneath hues so warm,
With the oak's charm, they find their form.

Laughing Hearts in the Understory

In the depths where the ferns softly sway,
A gathering of critters are at play,
'Did you hear that joke about the twig?'
A raccoon snickers, feeling quite big.

The hedgehog rolls in a fit of glee,
'It's not a twig, it's just a key!'
They chortle and chuckle; the shadows blend,
A party of pals, joy knows no end.

A sleepy owl hoots, 'What's that racket?'
A mouse squeaks back, 'It's our fun packet!'
The laughter echoes through roots so deep,
Tickling the soil, waking up sleep.

In this underworld of leafy delight,
Each chuckle and snicker shines ever bright,
Together they weave a tapestry bold,
Where laughter grows like stories untold.

The Jocular Journey of the Oak

Not so far from the grassy trail,
Where mossy rocks tell tales of the vale,
The oak sets out with a hearty cheer,
Proclaiming, 'Watch out, I'm coming near!'

Squirrels hop on from branch to branch,
'Can you catch us? Let's take a chance!'
The oak just shakes with a playful heart,
'Oh, my dear friends, I'm quite the art!'

A parade of ants march single file,
'We're stronger together, let's walk in style!'
The oak erupts in a rumbling laugh,
'You tiny marvels make quite the gaffe!'

With every twist of the winding route,
The laughter lingers, resolute,
Together they wander, jesters in leaf,
Making memories beyond belief.

The Tree's Whimsical Voice

In the breeze, the branches sway,
Leaves giggle as they dance and play.
Squirrels chatter with their nutty cheer,
The oak hums softly, lending an ear.

Beneath the boughs, shadows twist and twirl,
With every rustle, secrets unfurl.
A pinecone plops, makes a splat,
Who knew trees could be such a brat?

The sunlight tickles the bark's old face,
As dandelion wishes float with grace.
An acorn jokes, "I've got roots for you!",
While moss smiles, saying, "Let's grow anew!"

When autumn calls, the leaves fall down,
Like giggling kids, without a frown.
In nature's jest, we find our bliss,
The tree's voice sings; we can't resist.

Rejoicing in the Rustic Realm

In meadows where butterflies flit and zoom,
The grass tickles toes, so soft as a plume.
A rabbit hops, with a grin so wide,
While the daisies dance, filled with pride.

With every bloom, the daisies tease,
A crow caws from the top of the trees.
"Why did the bee stay out all night?",
"Looking for honey? Oh, what a sight!"

The brook bubbles on with a cheeky flow,
"I'm the best singer that you'll ever know!"
Laughter echoes through fields so bright,
As fireflies wink into the night.

In this rustic realm, where joy takes flight,
Each creature plays, from dawn until night.
Nature rejoices with every small jest,
In this fun-filled haven, we're truly blessed.

Jests in the Leaves

Upon a branch, the critters convene,
With slingshot nuts, they're a lively scene.
A leaf whispers, "Watch out for that one!",
As acorns are shot, oh, what fun!

The wind carries laughter through trees so merry,
Tickling the branches, making them cheery.
The shadows play tag; the sun joins in,
While beetles roll berries—who'll win this spin?

From trunk to treetop, the jests unfold,
In whispers of rustles, secrets are told.
"Why did the twig break up with the tree?",
"Because it found another limb more free!"

In the canopy's heart, life's such a hoot,
Where every verse feels like a playful root.
Among jests in the leaves, laughter blooms,
In nature's choir, joy brightly looms.

The Quirky Quotient of Nature

In the garden, where oddities thrive,
A gnarled old gnome does a silly jive.
Flowers gossip; bees start to tease,
"Buzz off for a while! Give us some ease!"

A hedgehog thinks he's a mighty knight,
While the wildflowers cheer him with delight.
"What's the hedgehog's secret to staying spry?",
"Spikes for chairs, oh me, oh my!"

The squirrels hold council, plotting a plan,
To steal from the birdfeeder: oh, what a scan!
"Don't wake the cat!" whispers the crowd,
With giggles and winks, all seem so proud.

In this quirky world, with glad-hearted things,
Where laughter and nature give joy in springs.
The trees stand tall, nature's wild whim,
We find ourselves chuckling, no need to swim.

The Jest of the Green Giants

In the shade of wide branches, they chatter,
Acorns drop like jokes, all in good banter.
One trunk tells a tale of a squirrel's dance,
While the others chuckle, caught in a trance.

A breeze whispers secrets, leaves tickle the bark,
A woodpecker tickles, it's quite a lark.
Each knot in the grain holds a story or two,
They giggle at storms, as if nature's a zoo.

The sun peeks through branches, a spotlight divine,
Pine needles join in, they sway in a line.
Each shadow a jest, every rustle a cheer,
The giants of green whisper, "Oh dear, oh dear!"

With laughter like thunder, they stand tall and proud,
Their roots spread wide, like jokes in a crowd.
Nature's own jesters, they dance in delight,
Amidst all the chaos, they shine ever bright.

Oak-Leaf Laughter

Leaves flutter and giggle, a rustling song,
Each leaf a comedian, where nothing's wrong.
An acorn shimmies, dressed up for the show,
"Why did the tree laugh?" they wink, "Don't you know?"

The breeze joins the jest, with a whoosh and a sigh,
Sending pinecone props spinning up to the sky.
Bark chuckles softly, a wise old sage,
As young saplings giggle, writing humor on a page.

The sun casts warm beams, a spotlight on greens,
While the critters don costumes, peeking between scenes.

It's a circus of nature, with laughter so pure,
The whole forest joins in, chortling for sure.

So gather round closely, and lend an ear wide,
To the tales of the woods and the fun they provide.
An oak's hearty laugh, an adventure in cheer,
Echoes through the woodland, vibrant and clear.

Revelry Among the Roots

Beneath gnarled old trunks, a party ensues,
Worms wearing top hats, sipping on dew.
Ladybugs waltz, twirling leaves in the air,
While mushrooms provide an odd dance floor flair.

"What's black and white and loved by the grove?"
A wise centipede rolls, as they share the joke's trove.
The roots intertwine like laughter shared tight,
Tickling the soil, under stars shining bright.

With each gentle gust, a cheer rises up,
Dance beats from crickets in rhythm and sup.
Flashing fireflies whirl, lights buzzing around,
Nature's own festival, laughter unbound.

Around every bough, a new joke is spun,
"Why did the tree join the band? For the fun!"
The revelry echoes through moonlit glades,
Roots deep in the ground, a party that swayed.

Charms of the Sturdy Sentinel

The sturdy oak stands, with a grin on its face,
Guarding the forest with style and grace.
"Why is life so knotty?" it chuckles with glee,
As squirrels nod knowingly, clutching their tea.

Its branches stretch wide, like arms in a hug,
While vines sneak in, giving each other a tug.
A canopy of laughter, both warm and bright,
Each sunbeam that filters feels just right.

A toad joins the fun, croaking silly rhymes,
While whispers of wind play with fun-loving chimes.
"What's a tree's favorite drink?" a young sprout asks aloud,
"Root beer!" echoes back, from the heart of the crowd.

The sentinel chuckles, its leaves quivering bliss,
For humor is evergreen, it can't be dismissed.
In this realm of wonder where trees laugh and spin,
Nature's own comedy, let the fun begin!

Musings from the Majestic Oak

Beneath my branches wide and grand,
   I hear the chatter, oh so bland.
A squirrel's gossip, a bird's complaint,
   Nature's humor is quite quaint.

The wind whispers secrets from afar,
   While sunbeams chuckle like a star.
A leaf drops down with a playful spin,
   Nature's laughter echoes within.

In acorn caps, I've seen them grin,
   As each nutty creature dives right in.
They scurry about with silly cheer,
   Making mischief linger near.

So here I stand, old and wise,
Watching antics with watchful eyes.
In this wild comedy, I play my part,
The oak's embrace warms every heart.

Chuckles in the Sun-Dappled Glade

In the glade where the sunbeams play,
Laughter skips from day to day.
With toadstools frolicking in a row,
And tickled leaves that dance to and fro.

The rabbit hops with a comical twist,
While butterflies flirt, they can't resist.
A chipmunk cracks jokes under a stone,
As daisies giggle, not alone.

The brook gurgles with a merry tune,
While frogs croak jokes beneath the moon.
Every shadow holds a silly tale,
In this glade where laughs prevail.

So come, dear friends, and join the cheer,
In this lively space where joy is clear.
Here in the sun-dappled fun we find,
A whimsical dance for heart and mind.

Jolly Secrets of the Sylvan Space

In the woods where whispers weave,
Jolly secrets twirl and cleave.
A mushroom winks, a fox rolls by,
Underneath the big blue sky.

A bug in shades looks oh so slick,
With tiny shades, the fashion click.
A tree stump laughs at its own height,
In the glimmers of morning light.

The owls hoot with a knowing glance,
While fireflies glow, they start to dance.
Every rustle brings a giggle near,
In this sylvan space of cheer.

So take a moment, pause your pace,
Join in the fun of this lively space.
With jolly vibes and laughter grand,
In the woods, you'll understand.

Humor Amidst the Verdant Giants

Amidst the giants standing tall,
Nature's jokes are best of all.
A raccoon with a playful jest,
Makes every wanderer feel blessed.

The sun peeks through with a cheeky grin,
As shadows laugh at where they've been.
A vine plays tag with passing bees,
While birds crack up in the leafy trees.

Down by the roots, worms tell tales,
Of what happens when mischief fails.
Every critter has stories to share,
In this vibrant space, there's joy to spare.

So join the fun, let laughter soar,
Amongst the giants, come explore.
In this theater of nature's embrace,
Find humor in every place.

The Wisecrack of the Wind

The wind whispers tales, quite absurd,
Of squirrels that dance, so unheard.
They twirl and they leap, what a sight,
As branches applaud in delight.

With every soft breeze, laughter is spun,
From acorns that joke, just out for fun.
Leaves giggle and chatter, bright and spry,
The wind winks and swirls, oh my, oh my!

Each gust carries whispers, secrets to keep,
Of owls who wear glasses and never sleep.
The trees shake their limbs, chuckles abound,
Where humor and joy are always found.

So come hear the mirth, let worries take flight,
In the rustling trees where all feels right.
As laughter cascades through the forest wide,
The wisecrack of the wind is our guide.

Tricks of the Timber

Beneath the boughs, there's mischief in play,
With creatures conspiring throughout the day.
A raccoon in shades, sly as a fox,
Steals snacks from the picnic, oh what a hoax!

The branches extend, like hands in a jest,
As birds crack the code, with songs that impress.
While shadows of squirrels dart left and right,
They pull off their pranks, oh what a sight!

Barking with laughter, the trunks stand so tall,
Always in on the joke, never too small.
The canopy chuckles, leaves dance in mirth,
Celebrating tricks that bring joy to the earth.

So heed the call of the timber so wise,
With each playful whisper beneath sunny skies.
For in every creak and every soft crunch,
Lies the humor of life, a delightful punch.

Revelations from the Revered Roots

Deep down below, where the secrets do dwell,
Roots whisper stories, oh what a swell!
A turtle with glasses reads books with glee,
Teaching wisdom to all, under the old tree.

With laughter they share, the tales of the old,
Of brambles and thickets, of adventures bold.
The ants take notes, and bees hum along,
Creating the rhythm of life's silly song.

These roots throw a party, a fest of delight,
With fungi and moss in a dance every night.
The mushrooms all laugh as they sway with the breeze,
In this underground world, they do just as they please.

Revealing the magic in each twist and turn,
Where humor and wisdom both giggle and yearn.
So listen closely, and you might just hear,
The reveling roots whispering, "Don't you fret, dear!"

The Silly Symphony of the Trees

In the forest of giggles, a concert unfolds,
With branches that sway, and laughter retold.
Brought to life by the winds' playful tease,
The trees form a band, oh what a breeze!

The oaks on the left bring a beat that's divine,
While spruces hum chords in a grand intertwine.
Pine cones roll in, keeping time like a drum,
While the willows spin tales, where no one is glum.

The leaves shimmy and shake, they dance with delight,
While branches throw parties that last through the night.
A symphony silly, where laughter's the score,
Each note a reminder, we always want more.

So gather around, let the music surround,
In the silly symphony, joy can be found.
With trees as our chorus, let worries take flight,
In this woodland orchestra, all feels just right.

Chortles Among the Boughs

The squirrels chatter and squeak,
As acorns drop down with a peek.
A crow makes a joke, but oh, what a flap!
While the shy rabbit chuckles, curled up for a nap.

Trees sway with laughter, leaves shake in delight,
While branches giggle, all through the night.
A woodpecker's tap dances with cheer,
In this wacky woodland, joy draws near.

A chipmunk slips on a slick, muddy floor,
And the owls hoot with laughter, wanting more.
The breeze whispers puns to the sunlit ground,
In this forest of fun, hilarity's found.

So come join the revelry, join in the spree,
Where laughter is free beneath every tree.
With nature's own humor, life finds its way,
In a world where we chuckle and play every day.

Merrymaking in the Meadow

In a field where daisies dance with the breeze,
A fox tells a tale that brings all to their knees.
The sun's golden rays wink down from above,
As butterflies flutter with laughter and love.

A cow moos a joke that gets all in a spin,
While sheep share their secrets with a mischievous grin.
The flowers all giggle, petals twinkling bright,
As crickets compose a symphony of light.

A ladybug slips on a dew-kissed leaf,
While rabbits chuckle, caught up in their grief.
But laughter's contagious; they soon join the fun,
In this meadow of mirth, the day's just begun.

So let's prance through the daisies, and laugh till we tire,
In this cheerful patch where smiles never expire.
With every small jest, the world seems to glow,
In the merrymaking meadow, where happiness flows.

Humor in the Grove

Among ancient trunks, with bark so wise,
The creatures exchange hearty alibis.
A parrot squawks riddles, a fox makes a face,
While a turtle, so slow, joins the jovial race.

A chipmunk slips by, raiding a stash,
While owls look down with a knowing flash.
Branches creak gently, trees join the jest,
As laughter erupts in this vibrant nest.

The sunlight peeks through, casting silly shadows,
While beetles parade in their glossy gallows.
A frog croaks a pun, and the crickets all rhyme,
In this grove filled with giggles, all lost track of time.

So gather your friends, let the chuckles ignite,
In this humor-filled haven, everything's right.
With every small quip, the joy multiplies,
In the rhythm of laughter, the spirit can rise.

The Banter of the Breeze

Whispers of humor swirl through the air,
As the wind tells a tale with a flick of its hair.
Leaves rustle softly, giving a cheer,
While nature joins in, spreading delight here.

A bee buzzing laughs, getting sticky with fun,
While the sky plays along, brightening the sun.
A chipper old oak cracks a wise little joke,
As flowers throw petals, a colorful cloak.

Clouds drift along, joining in on the fun,
Casting silly shapes that dance in the sun.
A gust of fresh air tickles a tail,
Making all creatures tell tales without fail.

So listen closely, let laughter take wing,
For the breeze has a way of making us sing.
With every soft giggle, our worries can freeze,
In the joyous embrace of the banter of breeze.

Laughing Leaves

In the breeze the leaves all chuckle,
As squirrels plot a nutty hustle.
They jest of acorns, mischief schemes,
And giggle softly in the beams.

A robin sings of silly fights,
While shadows dance through sunny lights.
The oak stands tall, a wise old fool,
Who's seen all pranks from every school.

Beneath the boughs, the laughter swells,
As whispers glide like playful spells.
The branches shake with every joke,
In leafy realms where spirits poke.

At twilight's call, the fireflies wink,
And in the dusk, the branches link.
They weave their tales in glowing threads,
Where merriment and mischief spreads.

The Jester's Grove

In this crazy grove of glee,
A jester hides, just wait and see.
He juggles nuts with silly flair,
While critters watch, their eyes laid bare.

A fox trots by with sly delight,
Two raccoons share a cake-sized bite.
They laugh about the things they've done,
Like stealing food and having fun.

The jester tosses leaves like confetti,
While trees sway gently, ever ready.
Each rustle holds a punchline true,
In nature's joke, we're all the crew.

As dusk descends with playful sighs,
The jester winks, his laughter flies.
In the grove, the joy won't end,
For every leaf is a merry friend.

Secrets of the Ancient Tree

An ancient tree with wisdom vast,
Holds secrets from the ages past.
It whispers tales of dreams and pranks,
Of playful spirits in its flanks.

The bark it wears, a grinning face,
Worn smooth from time and nature's grace.
Its roots entangle fables old,
Of mischief making, brave and bold.

A squirrel slips and tugs a vine,
The ground shakes with a laugh divine.
The tree just shakes its leafy head,
And shares the words the fox once said.

As twilight turns the sky to blue,
The tree laughs on, and so do you.
For every branch is filled with cheer,
And ancient secrets linger near.

Mischief Among the Branches

High above, the branches sway,
In leafy realms where squirrels play.
They plot a heist of nuts and seeds,
With cheeky grins and daring deeds.

The chipmunks laugh in organized chaos,
As everyone joins in, they'll pay us.
With sneaky hops and tumbles swift,
Each little friend, a mischief gift.

The leaves gossip in rustling tones,
About the antics of woodland drones.
Each whisper carries a giggle light,
In this fun-filled, starry night.

When morning breaks, the laughter remains,
In nature's heart, where joy retains.
So come and play among the trees,
Where mischief dances in the breeze.

www.ingramcontent.com/pod-product-compliance
Lightning Source LLC
Chambersburg PA
CBHW071844160426
43209CB00003B/402